BECOMING
YOU

Become The Person You Were Meant to Be

Robert C. Bachinger

PERFORMANCE
PUBLISHING

Contents

What I Mean by "Becoming You"

"Becoming you" is a process of self-discovery and personal growth in which you will explore your values, beliefs, and desires in order to develop a true sense of identity. "Becoming you" helps you to embrace your individuality and the unique qualities that make you who you are.

The process involves more than just your values, beliefs, and desires; it consists of discovering your strengths, weaknesses, passions, and interests and using them to shape your life and relationships. You will need to self-reflect and be willing to explore your inner self. It will involve learning to be authentic and genuine to yourself, even if you face pressure or expectations from others. It also involves accepting yourself for who you are without judgment or criticism.

Ultimately, this book is for anyone who wants to learn about what it means to grow. Growth should be a lifelong process. We, as children, grow automatically. I have five young grandchildren –

John (JR), Carson (Cam), Quinn (Bear), Benson (Hansie), and Giuliana (G Marie). Being around them helps me understand that for them, growth happens every day. Everything they experience is about growth, and we, as parents and grandparents, give them the latitude for this growth to happen (as long as they don't hurt themselves).

We stop thinking about our growth opportunities when we get into our later years. "Why?" you may ask. You see, most adult humans have an innate desire to be comfortable. We want to feel relaxed and at ease, which leads to a sense of contentment and satisfaction. Our stress levels reduce, and we are less anxious and worried. We enjoy our surroundings and experiences.

On the positive side, comfort is good for physical and mental health. It helps us sleep better and be more relaxed with less tension. Negatively, however, we become complacent and resist change or new experiences. Comfort can lead to a lack of personal growth and development.

Negatively, however, we become complacent and resist change or new experiences. Comfort can lead to a lack of personal growth and development.

I have met many people over the years who have set aside personal growth for the status quo –

people who are resistant to change and don't like to encounter new things. They are completely content doing the same thing over and over again. Some have good jobs, good friends, and good lives. Yet there seems to be something missing.

"Personal Growth"

Personal growth is the process of improving oneself in various areas of life. This can include improving one's physical, mental, and emotional well-being, as well as developing new skills and abilities. It is an ongoing journey that requires commitment and dedication, but the rewards are well worth the effort.

Personal growth is not always easy, and there will be setbacks and challenges along the way. However, it is important to remember that growth is not a destination but a journey.

This book is for those who may at one time have had this mindset and forgotten what that feeling was like. It is also for those searching for something that will help them feel deeply about themselves but who haven't gotten there yet.

> It doesn't matter where you are in life. You should want to continue to grow till the day you leave this earth.

It doesn't matter where you are in life. You should want to continue to grow till the day you leave this earth.

HELPFUL QUESTIONS TO REFLECT UPON:

1. What about where you are now makes you feel at ease or comfortable?
2. What things do you often do to learn more or get better at something?
3. What can you do to keep your mind and body healthy and ready for personal growth?
4. Can you describe how you see yourself right now?
5. How often do you push yourself to do things that might be a bit scary or difficult, and what things, if any, make this harder for you?

"If you're coasting, you're either losing momentum or else you're headed downhill."
–Joan Welsh

Chapter 1

"THIS IS THE STORY OF ME"

My story began on October 17th, 1961. It was a Tuesday. I was the last to be born to two immigrant parents, John and Maria. I had two brothers, John and Michael, and one sister, Anna, all several years older than me. My brothers always kidded me, saying I was "An Accident." I don't believe in accidents! Everyone has a purpose, a reason for being. You must discover why you were born and develop that WHY to become the best you.

> Everyone has a purpose, a reason for being. You must discover why you were born and develop that WHY to become the best you.

My childhood was not typical for the times because my parents came from a different country and a different culture. They were trying to adapt to their new surroundings, learn a new language, find work, and develop new relationships.

For me, though, the fact that my two brothers were six and five years older than me was a disadvantage in creating a deep connection with them. I did in later years, but that only happened once we were adults. Most of the time, I felt lost and alone because I never fit into their lives. They didn't want me around when they were running around with their buddies.

My sister was a bit closer in age, only three years separating us, but she did things that girls do, and that was not what I wanted to do. She liked playing with dolls, and I enjoyed playing with trucks and marbles and getting dirty.

Another aspect of our lives was that we didn't have a lot. My father found a job in 1957 working for a manufacturing company (from which he retired after 41 years). Still, at the time, it didn't pay enough to provide for our growing family. When I came around, we were living in a five-room 816-square-foot house, which was little space for us, but we made it work. My dad was always working, and I did not see him very much when I was growing up. He helped one of his co-workers paint houses in the summer, and in the winter, he fixed and installed furnaces and played in an ethnic band on the weekends.

Mom, on the other hand, was always home. She was the nurturer, the disciplinarian, and the person who cared for all our needs. She had difficulty with the English language and, at one point, was asked by the school to stop using her native language and speak English to my brothers because they were having difficulties communicating in school.

As my brothers, sister, and I grew older, Mom eventually became skillful in and studied cosmetology, going on to become a licensed beautician. Because of her ability, Dad and Mom decided to purchase a new house and convert the basement into a beauty shop for my mom to create her own business. We kids also welcomed the move as we could have a larger house and a bigger yard and be around more kids our age.

In my early years, my mom sent me to school earlier than she should have (looking back, I was 5.8 years old). In the late '60s, if you turned six before October 31st, you could enter your child into first grade; preschool and kindergarten were optional then. For my mom, it seemed like the right thing to do, but it turned out that I had many difficulties during my school years. Most of the children I would be with through my entire time at school would be older than me. My maturity level would be different from theirs – physically, mentally, and emotionally.

I was extremely outgoing and social. I would disrupt the class, and as a daydreamer, my short attention span often got me into trouble. My teachers would send notes home to my mom, telling her I needed to listen to instructions and pay attention better. That would continue for several years but would lessen as I matured. I never received good marks in class and struggled with just trying to live up to the standards of the time.

Junior high school was difficult for me. In the latter years, I decided to give sports a shot. In seventh grade, I tried out for the basketball team and didn't pass the tryouts. During the summer between seventh and eighth grades, I played baseball (the Pony League). I don't know why I didn't play Little League – maybe it was because my parents were unaware it was available. I probably came home one day and told my mom that my friend Tom, the next-door neighbor, was going to play and asked if I could. My brothers never were interested in sports; they wanted to make money and became caddies at the local country club.

Baseball was always my favorite sport, and I was good at it. But when I started playing football in eighth grade, things got tough. I wasn't as mature as the other kids, and I was only 4 feet 11 inches tall. In our team photo, you'd see me in the back row with the big guys, and I was much shorter than everyone else. I made the team, but I never played in a game that year.

When summer came, I returned to playing baseball, at which I excelled. The thing was, I was scared of getting hit by the ball, so my batting wasn't great. They asked me to try out for the all-star team at the end of the season. I gave it my best shot but ended up being one of the last kids to get cut from the team. The coach even picked his son over me. I'm not saying I shouldn't have been cut, but it felt like no one was looking out for me. I didn't have a mentor or anyone to look up to, which got me down. After that, I didn't want to play school sports anymore. I felt too hurt.

Little did I know that I would have a growth spurt by tenth grade and be 6 feet 2 inches tall!

High school wasn't any easier for me; my grades suffered, and my confidence waned. I remember that in ninth grade, my English teacher embarrassed me in front of the whole class. She made me stand in the hall until the period was over. All the trauma to which I was subjected during my sports endeavor and now in the classroom was taking its toll on me. Tenth grade was pivotal because I realized I was not cut out for regular school.

I knew that college was not in my future. First, my parents didn't have the money to send me to college; second, if they did have the money, I would have wasted it. I then searched for another avenue because I knew that I needed to. I found another path – vocational school. My father worked in manufacturing (metal stamping), and that's the path I decided to take. I researched the metal stamping industries and found a couple of vocations I could attain – I could work in a machine shop or do welding. I chose to weld.

Now the stigma in those days was that if you went to vocational school, you were looked down upon. You didn't have what it took to complete high school and make something of yourself. I believe that still exists today to a lesser degree. But completing eleventh and twelfth grades in a vocational school meant I could meet my schooling requirements and have a career. I also learned that the vocational school would help students find a job in their field of study. As I said earlier, tenth grade was a pivotal time for me. Choosing to change schools was a first step in me believing in myself. I was with individuals with similar interests, and I could be myself. I did excel in the welding class; I did better in English and Social Studies as well, although they were still a struggle.

During my senior year, the school set up interviews with multiple companies. I was hired at Range One Inc. to weld tubing for the four-wheel drive industries. I was using a different type of welding than I was taught, which was a challenge, but it was something I picked up quickly. I graduated on June 2nd, 1979, from the Mahoning County Joint Vocational School with a two-year welding degree and from Austintown Fitch High School with my high school diploma.

I became a valuable employee of Range One. I was quickly placed into a managerial role, managing the shop and job process. My pay rate did not reflect my ascension in the company, so in October of 1980, my father got me an interview with Compco Metal Products, and I was hired. On November 17th, 1980, I started my career as a laborer and doubled my pay rate. I knew I would have to wait for a welding position to become available before I could pursue that.

My career at Compco has been quite rewarding. The welding position never materialized, and I decided to learn as much as possible about the company. Looking below at my experience, you'll notice that I grew significantly in my career.

- From November 1980 to January 1984: General Laborer. I performed general laborer duties on the shop floor. I worked on machines, swept the floor, made boxes, and did whatever the foreman needed.

- From February 1984 to March 1988: Assistant Foreman. I assisted in the production-related processes on the shop floor. For this position, I was asked to relinquish my role in the shop and help my father run the plant and work on and learn the new computer system they were installing.

- From March 1988 to August 1990: Foreman. I was in charge of all production-related processes on the shop floor.

- From September 1990 to March 2002: Manager of Quality Control. I oversaw all quality processes and the development of ISO Certification. I was also in charge of administrating and developing the company's computer system. The computer system was easy for me to understand. We planned to move from a mainframe computer system to a Windows-based network. I was tasked with installing a local area network (so all the PCs could talk to each other) and a server to house the Enterprise Resource Planning (ERP) system, which would become the system that runs our company.

- From March 2002 to April 2010: Chief Information Officer. I continued developing the current ERP system and overseeing all the IT processes. I also became an officer of the company. I was put on the Board and given the title of Director.
- From May 2010 to July 2011: Vice President of Human Resources and Chief Culture Officer. In this role, I was tasked with creating a Strengths-Based Organization.
- From July 2011 to March 2013: Vice President of Quality Control. I oversaw the ISO Quality Control process.
- From March 2013 to May 2018: Vice President of Information Technologies. For this position, I oversaw the ERP system and the networking operation.

With my current title of Vice President of Corporate Safety and Training, I am responsible for all aspects of safety, and I oversee all the company's training activities.

The chapter you just finished reading is all about how I figured out who I am. It's pretty detailed and has a lot to think about. But it's important to understand this part of my life because it made me who I am now.

Every choice I made, every step I took, and every tough thing I got through has added a piece to the puzzle of me. All these pieces put together make up who I am, and I hope that the lessons I've learned might help you too. My story is unique, like everyone's is. But even though it's just about me, it can still connect with others. It's all about the challenges we face, the things we love, and never giving up. We all have the power to make our way in the world, driven by what we love and our determination to succeed.

Everyone has their struggles and wins, their dreams and goals. Even though these journeys are personal, they share something in common: our passions and determination shape who we are and the stories we tell.

As you read my story, you might see some parts that remind you of your own. I hope that you'll feel inspired by my story — not to do exactly what I did, but to keep going on your journey, guided by your passions and the drive to keep pushing forward.

HELPFUL QUESTIONS TO REFLECT UPON:

1. What do you often dream or think about doing in your future?
2. What plan do you have to make your life goals come true?
3. What kind of hard work are you ready to do to make your dreams happen, and what might this look like?
4. How do you like to learn best, and how does it help you in your life or work?
    a. If by watching, can you talk about a time when seeing something helped you learn or do something?
    b. If by listening, can you share a time when hearing something helped you learn or achieve something?
    c. If by doing, can you remember a time when doing something yourself helped you learn or get something done?
    d. If by reading/writing, can you talk about when reading or writing something was important for your learning or getting a job done?

Chapter 2

YOUR "WHY" AND
WHY IT MATTERS

Your "Why" refers to your purpose, motivation, or reason for doing something. It is the thing that drives you to act and pursue your goals.

Each person's "Why" is unique and can be influenced by their values, beliefs, and experiences. Some people's "Why" may be to positively impact the world, while others may be motivated by personal fulfillment or success. Your "Why" is the most important thing you can find out about yourself. It is the very essence of your being; why you are placed on this earth. It will be the difference between working in an average job, making ends meet, and working the most fulfilling career you could ever imagine.

Developing your "Why" is discovering and defining the purpose or motivation behind your actions and goals. It involves understanding what truly matters and aligning your actions with those values and beliefs.

One way to develop your "Why" is to engage in self-reflection. This can include journaling, meditating, or talking with a trusted friend or therapist about your values, beliefs, and goals. It can also involve exploring different areas of interest, trying new activities, and experimenting with different ways of living. Through this process, you can identify patterns and themes that are most important to you.

Another way to develop your "Why" is to seek role models or mentors who embody the values and beliefs you wish to emulate. Observing and learning from these individuals can give insights into how they conduct their lives and what drives them. Setting and achieving small, manageable goals can also help develop your "Why." Focusing on progress over perfection can build momentum and confidence to achieve larger goals that align with your values and beliefs.

Ultimately, developing your "Why" is a lifelong process. It requires continuous self-reflection, experimentation, and learning. Still, through this process, you can better understand yourself and what truly matters to you, leading to greater fulfillment and satisfaction.

> Ultimately, developing your "Why" is a lifelong process. It requires continuous self-reflection, experimentation, and learning.

As you saw in the previous chapter, during my years with Compco Industries, I have learned as much as possible about everything I could within the company, depending on my position. That was a way to make myself valuable.

I found my "Why" between 2002 and 2010 when our owner and one of my mentors, Greg Smith, introduced Strengths 2.0 from Gallup. It's an assessment that gives your top five strengths. My five are Relator, Maximizer, Developer, Adaptability, and Responsibility. Looking back on my career, these five strengths gave me an understanding I never realized I possessed. At the time, being a Developer and Maximizer were my most noticeable strengths.

I've always loved helping people, especially when I worked in IT, which is all about computers and technology. In this job, your main task is to help customers with their tech problems. It is true most of the time, but it's different when you're in a small company with many other tasks that also need attention.

Even with that, my rule was always this: when my coworkers — my customers in this job — needed help, I'd stop what I was doing and help them because they needed their tech to work right so they could do their jobs well. If they're having problems, they can't improve their work.

So, it didn't matter what else I had to do. When my coworkers had tech problems, they became my top priority. Helping them return to their work was always the most important thing for me.

After understanding how strengths and strength-based leadership played into my success, I was determined to learn more. If I could understand all about strengths, I would be able to help others the way it helped me. Our organization has everyone participate in the Gallup Strengths 2.0 process. We even have pictures of all the employees on the wall, with their five strengths listed.

How Strengths Get More Engagement from People

"Strengths" is an approach that focuses on your strengths and positive qualities rather than your weaknesses or areas for improvement. The goal is to help team members build on their strengths — rather than trying to fix their weaknesses — to achieve better results and improve performance.

This approach is based on the idea that individuals are more likely to be motivated and engaged using their natural abilities and talents. Strength-based leaders aim to create a positive and supportive work environment that allows team members to thrive and reach their full potential.

In 2020, I took an assessment at the WHY Institute that spelled out my "Why" fully. Below are the results of the assessment.

MY WHY

"Contribute: I believe in contributing to a greater cause. I want to make a difference in the lives of others. I love to support others, and I relish success that leads to the greater good. I seek to add value in everything I do and am often referred to as the 'go-to' person." (https://whyinstitute.com/contribute/)

How do I live "My Why"?

"I am passionate about contributing to a cause bigger than myself."

I strive to contribute by something beyond personal interests or benefits. I find a deep sense of satisfaction and fulfillment in serving others or contributing to a cause that serves the greater good. It could involve environmental advocacy, social justice, community service, or any mission that transcends individual gains.

"My goal is to positively impact other people's lives."

My main objective is to influence others positively. It might mean offering kindness, providing assistance, spreading knowledge, or using my abilities to improve situations for others. Whether in one-on-one interactions or affecting many people, I aim to leave people better off than they were before they interacted with me.

"Supporting others and celebrating their success brings me joy."

I gain happiness not just from my accomplishments but from seeing others succeed. It could involve being a good listener, a motivator, a mentor, or simply being there for others in times of need. Other people's success does not threaten me; instead, I cheer for them and feel a sense of pride in their achievements, as if they were my own.

"I aim to make every action meaningful, often referred to as someone who adds value in all that I do."

I aim to ensure that my actions carry purpose and add value. I do not engage in tasks half-heartedly; instead, I commit fully to my actions, aiming to produce quality results. Being someone who "adds value" means I improve and enrich every situation or project I'm involved in, whether by bringing fresh insights, showing exemplary dedication, or improving the outcome. I am reliable, and people can count on me to contribute significantly.

This statement paints a picture of a selfless, goal-oriented, supportive, and dependable person. I strive to improve the world, one action at a time, by helping others and investing wholeheartedly in everything I do.

You see, over the years, I have been able to pursue my "Why" through different avenues.

In 2018 I went to Orlando and attended the International Maxwell Conference (IMC). I became a certified Speaker, Trainer, and Coach of the John Maxwell Team.

John Maxwell is a renowned author, speaker, and leadership expert. He is widely recognized as one of the foremost leadership and personal development authorities. John Maxwell's teachings and insights are rooted in the belief that everyone has the potential to become a leader and make a positive impact in their personal and professional lives. His work emphasizes the importance of character, integrity, continuous learning, and serving others as fundamental principles of effective leadership.

In 2019 I became a Ziglar Legacy Certified Coach.

Zig Ziglar began his career as a salesman for various companies before transitioning to a career as a motivational speaker and trainer. He traveled extensively, delivering powerful speeches and seminars on personal development, sales, and success principles. Ziglar's ability to connect with audiences and entertainingly give practical wisdom made him a highly sought-after speaker.

The Ziglar Legacy Certified Coach (ZLCC) program is a training and certification program offered by the Ziglar Corporation. The ZLCC program is designed for individuals passionate about personal development, coaching, and helping others achieve their goals.

These two certifications gave me a toolbox of multiple training programs to help me give others what they want.

As Zig Ziglar once said, 'You can get everything in life you want if you will just help enough other people get what they want.'

As you can see, this last quote embodies my quest fully.

> "If I have a part in making you successful, then
> I am successful. How can I help you?"
> –Robert C. Bachinger

HELPFUL QUESTIONS TO REFLECT UPON:

1. What things make you want to work hard or do well in your life or job?
2. What things do you believe in, and how do these things change what you do or decide?
3. Can you explain the main reason or purpose behind what you do?
4. How are you making your main purpose stronger and what are you doing to make it more important in your life?
5. What are you good at and how do these skills help you succeed?

"Find a job you enjoy doing, and you will
never have to work a day in your life."
–Mark Twain

Chapter 3

"BECOMING SUCCESSFUL!"

Becoming successful is a journey that requires determination, hard work, and a clear understanding of one's goals and aspirations. It is a process that requires setting objectives, creating a plan to achieve them, and then taking action to make that plan a reality.

Just like your "Why," success means different things to different people. For some, success may be achieving financial prosperity, while for others, it may be finding happiness and fulfillment in their personal lives. Regardless of how you define success, specific steps can be taken to increase the likelihood of achieving it.

One method is to use S.M.A.R.T. goals. Goals should be Specific, Measurable, Achievable, Relevant, and Time-bound. By setting S.M.A.R.T. goals, you can clearly understand what you want to accomplish and how you plan to do so.

Specific: Be precise and particular in the desired outcome of the goal!

Measurable: What measurements will track the progress of the goal?

Achievable: Is the goal realistic and attainable?

Relevant: Is the goal relevant to your success?

Time-bound: What is the timeframe for the success of the goal?

For goal setting to be successful, these elements need to exist.

Taking action is the next step in becoming successful. Staying focused, motivated, and willing to work hard and sacrifice to achieve your goals is essential. This may mean working extra hours, learning new skills, or assuming additional responsibilities. In addition to hard work and determination, becoming successful requires a positive attitude and adapting to change. Being open to new ideas and willing to take risks to achieve your goals is essential.

It is critical to develop a strong work ethic. Successful individuals are often characterized by their ability to work hard and consistently toward their goals. They understand that success requires effort and dedication and are willing to put in the time and energy necessary to achieve it.

Staying humble and always willing to learn, grow, and improve is essential. Successful individuals are always looking for ways to improve themselves and their skills. They are curious and open to new ideas and perspectives and understand that learning is lifelong.

> It is critical to develop a strong work ethic. Successful individuals are often characterized by their ability to work hard and consistently toward their goals.

Successful individuals tend to have a "can-do" attitude and believe in their ability to achieve their goals. They view challenges as opportunities for growth and learn from their mistakes. They surround themselves with positive influences. Successful individuals tend to have a robust support system of friends, family, and mentors who provide encouragement and guidance. They also tend to surround themselves with other successful and motivated individuals, which helps to keep them motivated and on track.

What is success? Success is not a destination but a journey. Success requires setting specific and measurable goals, developing a solid work ethic, continuously learning and growing, having a positive attitude and mindset, and surrounding oneself with positive influences. It is important to celebrate small victories along the way and acknowledge that there is always room for improvement. By following these steps and remaining dedicated and determined, you can increase your chances of achieving success.

HELPFUL QUESTIONS TO REFLECT UPON:

1. What is success to you?
2. Who is successful in your eyes, and what can you learn from them?
3. How do you incorporate discipline in creating and adhering to S.M.A.R.T. (Specific, Measurable, Achievable, Relevant, Time-bound) goals in your life?
4. How are you cultivating a strong work ethic that will contribute to your success?
5. In what ways are you seeking to connect with positive influencers, and how do you expect this to assist in your journey?

"Success is a state of mind. If you want success,
start thinking of yourself as successful."
–Dr. Joyce Brothers

Chapter 4

"OVERCOMING FAILURES"

Failure is a natural part of the journey toward success. It is often said that failure is a necessary precursor to success. Yet even though we all know this, it can still be tough to handle failure when it happens. It can feel like a crushing blow, a sign that we are not good enough or that our dreams and ambitions will fail. But the truth is, failure is simply a learning opportunity – a chance to grow and improve, and ultimately, to achieve our goals.

Failure is not the end of the road. It is simply a bump in the street, a setback that can be overcome. The key is to keep going and pushing forward, even in the face of adversity. This can be incredibly difficult, especially when we feel we have failed so completely that there is no way to recover. But the reality is that there is always a way forward, always a way to overcome our setbacks and achieve our goals.

Failure is a natural learning process. When we fail, we must examine what went wrong, what we could have done differently, and what we can learn from our mistakes. This valuable experience can help us grow and develop our skills so we can become better and more resilient in the face of future challenges.

One of the most famous examples of someone who refused to let failure stop them is Thomas Edison. He famously "failed" thousands of times before finally inventing the light bulb. When asked about his many shortcomings, he is said to have replied, "I have not failed. I've just found 10,000 ways that won't work."

This attitude is critical to overcoming failure. Rather than seeing loss as a personal defeat, it is essential to see it as a natural part of innovation and growth.

Failure should breed resilience. Resilience is the ability to bounce back from setbacks, recover from adversity, and keep going in the face of difficulty. Resilience is not something with which we are born, but we can develop it over time. This can be done through various techniques, such as practicing mindfulness, cultivating positive thinking, and building a solid support network.

Understanding that failure does not reflect our worth is also essential. It is easy to fall into the trap of thinking that our failures define us and are a sign of our weakness or lack of ability. But this is not true. Failure is a natural part of the journey toward success and does not define who we are.

Ultimately, the key to not letting failures stop you is to maintain a positive attitude, remain resilient in the face of adversity, and keep pushing forward, even when there is no hope. With time, effort, and dedication, anything is possible. So, if you have experienced failure, do not give up. Instead, use it as an opportunity to learn, grow, and become the best version of yourself that you can be. The journey toward success may be long and complex, but it is always worth it.

> Understanding that failure does not reflect our worth is also essential. It is easy to fall into the trap of thinking that our failures define us and are a sign of our weakness or lack of ability.

HELPFUL QUESTIONS TO REFLECT UPON:

1. How do you prepare yourself to cope with potential failures, and do you believe anyone can truly be ready for them?
2. How do you pick yourself up and respond after experiencing a failure?
3. How do you cultivate resilience and adaptability when confronted with failure?

"Failure is an event, not a person."
–Zig Ziglar

Chapter 5

"WHAT CAN YOU DO NEXT?"

As I review my work, what I have accomplished, and what I have yet to achieve, I'm proud and honored that I might make a difference in your life with my story. Becoming you is a lifelong journey of self-discovery and personal growth. Here are some steps to help you become more authentic and embrace who you are:

1. Reflect on your values and beliefs: Take time to identify your core values, the principles that guide your decisions and actions.
2. Explore your passions and interests: Engage in activities that bring you joy and fulfillment.
3. Embrace self-acceptance: Accept yourself as you are, including your strengths, weaknesses, and imperfections.
4. Seek self-awareness: Develop a deep understanding of who you are.

5. Surround yourself with supportive relationships: Cultivate relationships with people who accept and appreciate you for who you are.
6. Embrace personal growth and learning: Commit to lifelong learning and personal development.

The art of becoming you is in your hands! But it requires dedication, self-reflection, and a willingness to learn and grow. You have the power to shape your own identity and create the life you want, but it takes effort and perseverance to achieve your goals. Remember to be kind to others and yourself and seek support and guidance from those around you when you need it. The more you invest in it, the more you will reap the rewards of living a fulfilling and authentic life.

Live your best life!

How are you going to live your best life? Identify your values, passion, and purpose and align your decisions and actions around them. Embrace uncertainty and be open to new experiences and growth opportunities. But always stay true to who you are.

Strive to be the best possible version of yourself!

How you choose to live your life is up to you. Remember, there is always time to start making changes and pursue your 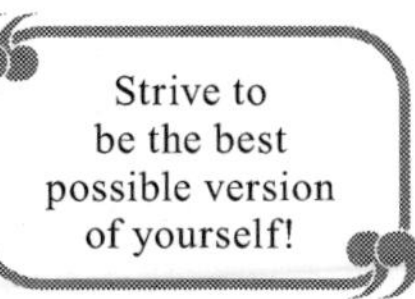 dreams. Don't let life's setbacks (and there will be setbacks) destroy your dreams and ambitions.

"Success is not final, failure is not fatal: it is
the courage to continue that counts."
–Winston S. Churchill

Remember, choose to grow over
being comfortable. It can and will
be tough but rewarding.

I believe in you! So, believe in yourself!

"Becoming You" is all in your hands.

Robert Bachinger is a seasoned professional with over 43 years of experience at Compco Industries. He strongly advocates strength-based leadership and understands the power of knowing your WHY. Robert firmly believes that knowing who you are and believing in yourself is the key to success.

Throughout his career, Robert has held various roles and has become a respected figure in the manufacturing industry. His deep understanding of Compco Industries has enabled him to provide invaluable insights and guidance, contributing significantly to the company's success. Robert's commitment to excellence has been a driving force behind many of Compco Industries' achievements. His ability to inspire and motivate others has created a positive and productive work environment.

Robert's passion for his profession is infectious, and his dedication to ongoing learning and development inspires those around him. He has left a lasting impact on Compco Industries, and his legacy will continue to influence future generations of professionals in the manufacturing industry.

Made in the USA
Monee, IL
07 July 2026

56546410R00028